Nonresistance: Cultivating Ahimsa for Harmony And Peace

Swami Vivekananda;
Institute for Thought & Philosophy

GRAPEVINE INDIA

Published by

GRAPEVINE INDIA PUBLISHERS PVT LTD

www.grapevineindia.com
Delhi | Mumbai
email: grapevineindiapublishers@gmail.com

Ordering Information:
Quantity sales: Special discounts are available on quantity
purchases by corporations, associations, and others.
For details, reach out to the publisher.

First published by Grapevine India 2023
Copyright © Grapevine 2023

NON-RESISTANCE

I preach only the Upanishads. If you look, you will find that I have never quoted anything but the Upanishads. And of the Upanishads, it is only that One idea, strength. The quintessence of the Vedas and Vedanta and all lies in that one word. Buddha's teaching was non-resistance, or non-injury. But I think this is a better way of teaching the same thing. For behind that non-injury lay a dreadful weakness. It is weakness that conceives the idea of resistance. I do not think of punishing or escaping from a drop of sea-spray. It is nothing to me. Yet to the mosquito it would be serious. Now I would make all injury like that.

*

In reading the Bhagavad-Gita, many of you in Western countries may have felt astonished at the second chapter, wherein Shri Krishna calls Arjuna a hypocrite and a coward because of his refusal to fight, or offer resistance, on account of his adversaries being his friends and relatives, making the plea that non-resistance was the highest ideal of love. This is a great lesson for us all to learn, that in all matters the two extremes are alike. The extreme positive and the extreme negative are always similar. When the vibrations of light are too slow, we do not see them, nor do we see them when they are too rapid. So with sound; when very low in pitch, we do not hear it; when very high, we do not hear it either. Of like nature is the difference between resistance and non-resistance. One man does not resist because he is weak, lazy, and cannot, not because he will not; the other man knows that he can strike an irresistible blow if he likes; yet he not only does not strike, but blesses his enemies. The one who from weakness resists not commits a sin, and as such cannot receive any benefit from the non-resistance; while the other would commit a sin by offering resistance.

Buddha gave up his throne and renounced his position, that was true renunciation; but there cannot be any question of renunciation in the case of a beggar who has nothing to renounce. So we must always be careful about what we really mean when we speak of this non-resistance and ideal love. We must first take care to understand whether we have the power of resistance or not. Then, having the power, if we renounce it and do not resist, we are doing a grand act of love; but if we cannot resist, and yet, at the same time, try to deceive ourselves into the belief that we are actuated by motives of the highest love, we are doing the exact opposite. Arjuna became a coward at the sight of the mighty array against him; his "love" made him forget his duty towards his country and king. That is why Shri Krishna told him that he was a hypocrite: Thou talkest like a wise man, but thy actions betray thee to be a coward; therefore stand up and fight!

*

The highest ideals are not for all. Non-resistance is not for the man who thinks the replacing of the maggot in the wound by the leprous saint with "Eat, Brother!" disgusting and horrible. Non-resistance is practised by a mother's love towards an angry child. It is a travesty in the mouth of a coward, or in the face of a lion.

*

We have only to grasp the idea of gradation of morality and everything becomes clear.

Renunciation — non-resistance — non-destructiveness — are the ideals to be attained through less and less worldliness, less and less resistance, less and less destructiveness. Keep the ideal in view and work towards it. None can live in the world without resistance, without destruction, without desire. The world has not come to that state yet when the ideal can be realised in society.

The progress of the world through all its evils making it fit for the ideals, slowly but surely. The majority will have to go on with this slow growth — the exceptional ones will have to get out to realise the idea in the present state of things.

*

The Gita opens with this very significant verse: "Arise, O Prince! Give up this faint-heartedness, this weakness! Stand up and fight!" Then Arjuna, trying to argue the matter [with Krishna], brings higher moral ideas, how non-resistance is better than resistance, and so on. He is trying to justify himself, but he cannot fool Krishna. Krishna is the higher Self, or God. He sees through the argument at once. In this case [the motive] is weakness. Arjuna sees his own relatives and he cannot strike them. …

There is a conflict in Arjuna's heart between his emotionalism and his duty. The nearer we are to [beasts and] birds, the more we are in the hells of emotion. We call it love. It is self-hypnotisation. We are under the control of our [emotions] like animals. A cow can sacrifice its life for its young. Every animal can. What of that? It is not the blind, birdlike emotion that leads to perfection. … [To reach] the eternal consciousness, that is the goal of man! There emotion has no place, nor sentimentalism, nor anything that belongs to the senses — only the light of pure reason. [There] man stands as spirit.

Now, Arjuna is under the control of this emotionalism. He is not what he should be — a great self-controlled, enlightened sage working through the eternal light of reason. He has become like an animal, like a baby, just letting his heart carry away his brain, making a fool of himself and trying to cover his weakness with the flowery names of "love" and so on. Krishna sees through that. Arjuna talks like a man of little learning and brings out many reasons, but at the same time he talks the language of a fool.

*

There have been three things in Buddhism: the Buddha himself, his law, his church. At first it was so simple. When the Master died, before his death, they said: "What shall we do with you?" "Nothing." "What monuments shall we make over you?" He said: "Just make a little heap if you want, or just do not do anything." By and by, there arose huge temples and all the paraphernalia. The use of images was unknown before then. I say they were the first to use images. There are images of Buddha and all the saints, sitting about and praying. All this paraphernalia went on multiplying with this organisation. Then these monasteries became rich. The real cause of the downfall is here. Monasticism is all very good for a few; but when you preach it in such a fashion that every man or woman who has a mind immediately gives up social life, when you find over the whole of India monasteries, some containing a hundred thousand monks, sometimes twenty thousand monks in one building — huge, gigantic buildings, these monasteries, scattered all over India and, of course, centres of learning, and all that — who were left to procreate progeny, to continue the race? Only the weaklings. All the strong and vigorous minds went out. And then came national decay by the sheer loss of vigour.

I will tell you of this marvellous brotherhood. It is great. But theory and idea is one thing and actual working is another thing. The idea is very great: practicing nonresistance and all that, but if all of us go out in the street and practice non-resistance, there would be very little left in this city. That is to say, the idea is all right, but nobody has yet found a practical solution [as to] how to attain it.

*

[The fanatical belief of many of these invaders into India is] that those who do not belong to their sect have no right to live. They will go to a place where the fire will never be quenched when they die; in this life they are only fit to be made into slaves or murdered; and that they have only the right to live as slaves to "the true believers", but never as free men. So in this way, when these waves burst upon India, everything was submerged. Books and literature and civilization went down.

But there is a vitality in that race which is unique in the history of humanity, and perhaps that vitality comes from non-resistance. Non-resistance is the greatest strength. In meekness and mildness lies the greatest strength. In suffering is greater strength than in doing.

In resisting one's own passions is far higher strength than in hurting others. And that has been the watchword of the race through all its difficulties, its misfortunes and its prosperity. It is the only nation that never went beyond its frontiers to cut the throats of its neighbours. It is a glorious thing. It makes me rather patriotic to think I am born a Hindu, a descendant of the only race that never went out to hurt anyone, and whose only action upon humanity has been giving and enlightening and purifying and teaching, but never robbing.

*

I once met a man in my country whom I had known before as a very stupid, dull person, who knew nothing and had not the desire to know anything, and was living the life of a brute. He asked me what he should do to know God, how he was to get free. "Can you tell a lie?" I asked him. "No," he replied. "Then you must learn to do so. It is better to tell a lie than to be a brute, or a log of wood. You are inactive; you have not certainly reached the highest state, which is beyond all actions, calm and serene; you are too dull even to do something wicked." That was an extreme case, of course, and I was joking with him; but what I meant was that a man must be active in order to pass through activity to perfect calmness.

Inactivity should be avoided by all means. Activity always means resistance. Resist all evils, mental and physical; and when you have succeeded in resisting, then will calmness come. It is very easy to say, "Hate nobody, resist not evil," but we know what that kind of thing generally means in practice. When the eyes of society are turned towards us, we may make a show of non-resistance, but in our hearts it is canker all the time. We feel the utter want of the calm of non-resistance; we feel that it would be better for us to resist.

If you desire wealth, and know at the same time that the whole world regards him who aims at wealth as a very wicked man, you, perhaps, will not dare to plunge into the struggle for wealth, yet your mind will be running day and night after money. This is hypocrisy and will serve no purpose. Plunge into the world, and then, after a time, when you have suffered and enjoyed all that is in it, will renunciation come; then will calmness come. So fulfil your desire for power and everything else, and after you have fulfilled the desire, will come the time when you will know that they are all very little things; but until you have fulfilled this desire, until you have passed through that activity, it is impossible for you to come to the state of calmness, serenity, and self-surrender. These ideas of serenity and renunciation have been preached for thousands of years; everybody has heard of them from childhood, and yet we see very few in the world who have really reached that stage. I do not know if I have seen twenty persons in my life who are really calm and non-resisting, and I have travelled over half the world.

*

The true man is he who is strong as strength itself and yet possesses a woman's heart. You must feel for the millions of beings around you, and yet you must be strong and inflexible and you must also possess Obedience; though it may seem a little paradoxical — you must possess these apparently conflicting virtues. If your superior order you to throw yourself into a river and catch a crocodile, you must first obey and then reason with him. Even if the order be wrong, first obey and then contradict it. The bane of sects, especially in Bengal, is that if any one happens to have a different opinion, he immediately starts a new sect, he has no patience to wait. So you must have a deep regard for your Sangha. There is no place for disobedience here. Crush it out without mercy. No disobedient members here, you must turn them out. There must not be any traitors in the camp. You must be as free as the air, and as obedient as this plant and the dog.

Milton Keynes UK
Ingram Content Group UK Ltd.
UKHW012143041223
433798UK00003B/72

9 789358 372724